天下泉城

中共济南市委政策研究室
济南市文化广电新闻出版局
济南出版有限责任公司

济南非物质文化遗产撷英

Collection of Intangible Cultural Heritage in Jinan

THE CITY OF SPRINGS

济南出版社

序 言

济南是一座具有两千六百多年建城史的历史文化名城，不仅留有丰富的物质文化遗存，而且拥有众多的非物质文化遗产。这些非物质文化遗产，生动记录了济南人民长期以来生产生活的习俗和民风，也充分体现了济南先民的文化智慧和高超技艺，是鲜活的地域文化的代表，也是不可复制的活的文化化石。

济南市委、市政府高度重视对非物质文化遗产的保护，在非遗项目的搜集、挖掘、整理、保护、传承、展示等方面做了大量卓有成效的工作，使这些鲜艳的文化奇葩得以培育和开放。用图片的方式整理和记录济南地区的非遗项目，让它得到生动展示和有效传承，是非遗保护的一项重要内容，也是历史和现实的迫切需要。这本图集选取了济南地区可以用图片展示的比较典型的五十八个非遗项目（包括一至三批全部国家级、省级和部分市级认定项目），对其产生发展历史、项目突出特点和现实传承状况进行了认真研究和生动展示，原汁原味地反映了这些项目的制作过程或表演场景，尽量为读者提供生动直观的文字和图片资料，力所能及地从不同侧面展现济南非遗项目的生存状态。

非物质文化遗产的保护和传承是一项长期的艰巨任务，既需要政府的积极引导和扶持，也需要社会各方面力量的参与和支持。希望能通过出版这本图片集，提高全社会对非遗事业的关注度和支持度，让非遗保护传承事业不断推向新的高度，让中华民族的文化传统传承下去，让这些老祖宗创造并世代传承的非物质文化遗产在新的时代发扬光大。

二〇一三年三月

目录

CONTENTS

傳統技藝

「传统技艺」 Traditional Crafts

東阿鎮「福牌」阿膠制作技藝

東阿鎮『福牌』阿膠制作技藝

Manufacture Craft of Fu Brand Donkey-hide Gelatin in Dong'e Town

省级非遗代表性传承人杨福安在检查产品

阿胶因产自平阴县东阿镇而得名，是由驴皮煎煮浓缩而成的固体胶。"福牌"阿胶由原"树德堂"、"怀德堂"、"太子衡老药店"等合并成的平阴阿胶厂（现山东福胶集团）生产，是国家级非遗项目。"福牌"阿胶的生产，环境独特、选料考究、遵古炮制、工序繁多，需经驴皮炮制、取汁煎胶、浓缩收胶、凝胶切胶、晾胶擦胶、印字包装等几十道工序方能完成，具有丰厚的技术内涵，蕴含着中华医药博大精深的历史文化价值。

As its name implies, ejiao originated from Dong'e Town of Jinan, which is a special solid gelatin that is made from donkey's hide with the reasonable decocting time and concentrating skill. As one of the state-level intangible cultural heritage projects, Fu Brand Donkey-hide Gelatin is produced in Pingyin Donkey-hide Gelatin Factory, or Fu Jiao Group, which is formed by three Chinese traditional pharmacies—Shu De Tang, Huai De Tang and Tai Zi Heng Pharmacy. While maintaining the integrity of the production processes is important, including processing, decocting, concentrating, congealing, airing and packaging, it is more so to blend the selected raw materials, the unique production environment and the heritage of processing craft to make the perfect donkey-hide gelatin. Therefore, this Chinese traditional medicine reflects its complex technical connotation and profound historical cultural value.

刮毛

切胶

挂旗

擦胶

晾胶

包装

济南烤鸭制作技艺

明末清初济南就有专门经营烤鸭的店家，姚焕金、张成祥多次去清宫内廷制作烤鸭，解放后济南烤鸭师傅多次给国家领导人和外宾制作表演，现为省级非遗项目。济南烤鸭均选用微山湖优质瘦型种鸭，制作中要先后经过宰杀、充气、放气、烫浇、挂晾、上色、晾干、入炉、调整等传统工序，烤出的鸭子外皮酥脆、肉质鲜嫩、味道鲜美、肥而不腻。

During the late Ming and early Qing dynasties, there were several roast duck restaurants specializing in roast duck in Jinan. Dated back to the Qing Dynasty, Yao Huanjin and Zhang Chengxiang as well-known chefs were invited to the court to make roast duck for the royal family. After the People's Republic of China was founded, the local famous chefs presented their skills of making the roast duck to our state leaders and foreigners more than once. This craft has been listed as one of the province-level intangible cultural heritage projects. The raw materials are high quality thin-type ducks that are cultivated in Weishan Lake which is the fifth largest fresh water lake in China. In order to roast a crispy, tender duck, just like other gourmet food, its making process requires nine steps at least, including cleaning, inflating, deflating, scalding, airing, coloring, drying, roasting and rolling before the duck can be served.

挂晾

烤 制

调 整

晾 干

片 切

成品和佐料

濟南油旋制作技藝

济南油旋制作技艺

The Craft of Youxuan in Jinan

油旋在济南已有100多年历史，是济南传统名优风味小吃，弘春美斋的油旋现为省级非遗项目。制作油旋要和软面，制成面剂儿擀成长条，抹上花生油和调味料，边抻拉边将面皮卷起，放鏊子上压成圆饼烙黄，再放入烤箱内慢火烤熟，用手指捅压成漩涡状。烤好的油旋皮酥瓢软、葱香浓郁、色泽金黄、造型美观，是老少咸宜的美食。

Youxuan is one of the famous traditional snacks of Jinan, which has been a long history of more than 100 years. Hongchunmeizhai's youxuan is one of the province-level intangible cultural heritage projects. Firstly, knead the soft dough, and then separate the dough into several equal pieces and roll into strips. Secondly, wipe peanut oil and flavorings over the surface of each strip. Stretch the strip and roll it up simultaneously, and then pat the small dough into a grigger on the griddle until it turns brown. Turn it over and brown the other side. Lastly, put the grigger into the oven under the low fire. When it is roasted, the craftsman pierces it with his finger. Incredibly, there is a spiral hole on its surface. Because it tastes crispy outside but soft inside with scallion's fragrance, youxuan is popular among all age groups.

省级非遗代表性传承人卢利华在操作油旋

烙 制

烤 制

 出 炉

成 品

仲宫白酒传统酿造技艺

仲宫白酒传统酿造技艺

Traditional Brewing Technique of Zhonggong Liquor

发酵

装甑

瓷缸存酒

灌 装

产 品

清代富泉酒店酿酒取水的古井

仲宫地区酿酒于汉代即已兴盛，现在的济南趵突泉酿酒公司继承了清代富泉酒家的传统酿造工艺，现为省级非遗项目。趵突泉酿酒公司利用仲宫独特的自然环境和气候条件，沿用三甑"粮渣"加一甑"回渣"、一甑"扔渣"的"老五甑"传统工艺，经过原辅材料筛选、粉碎、清蒸、润料、出池配料、开汽装甑、蒸煮蒸馏、出甑凉渣、入池发酵等十几道工序，生产全国驰名的趵突泉白酒。

It is said that the technique of making liquor in Jinan attained development and prosperity in the Han Dynasty. As one of the province-level intangible cultural heritage projects, Baotuquan Brewing Company inherited the traditional brewing technique of Fuquanjiujia that's a famous brewing workshop in the Qing Dynasty. The unique landscape, fine water quality, special soil, and the subtropical climate are natural advantages for brewing Baotuquan liquor. According to the inheritance and development of traditional technique, Baotuquan liquor is well-known throughout the country. It has preserved five complicated traditional distillation processes through screening grains, crushing grains, steaming grains, soaking grains, adjusting proportions, steaming and distilling, cooling the grain residue and fermenting.

石家老陶制作技艺

石家老陶制作技艺

Shijia Traditional Pottery

拉　坯　　　　　精　修

成　品

成　型　　　　　　　　　　　　烧　制

　　石家老陶源于具有四五千年历史的大汶口柞沟制陶工艺，上世纪80年代引入济南，现为省级非遗项目。石家老陶为纯手工制陶工艺，要经过制泥、拉坯、整形、打光、烧制、磨光等十几道工序，制作彩纹陶、开片陶、镶嵌陶、仿木陶四类陶器。石家老陶既认真继承不同时期的传统工艺，又善于不断创新改革发展，制品精到独特，具有极高的艺术价值。

Originated from Dawenkou zhegou during about 3000 BC, craft of Shijia traditional pottery which was introduced in Jinan during 1980s now is one of the province-level intangible cultural heritage projects. After over ten traditional manual processes, like preparing clay, jiggering, reshaping, polishing, firing and furbishing, Shijia traditional potting could take on four different appearances: stripe pottery, crackle pottery, inlaid pottery and wood-like pottery. Along with the inheritance and development of traditional technique, Shijia brings traditional pottery culture to the public, whose distinctive products are of high artistic value.

仿木陶

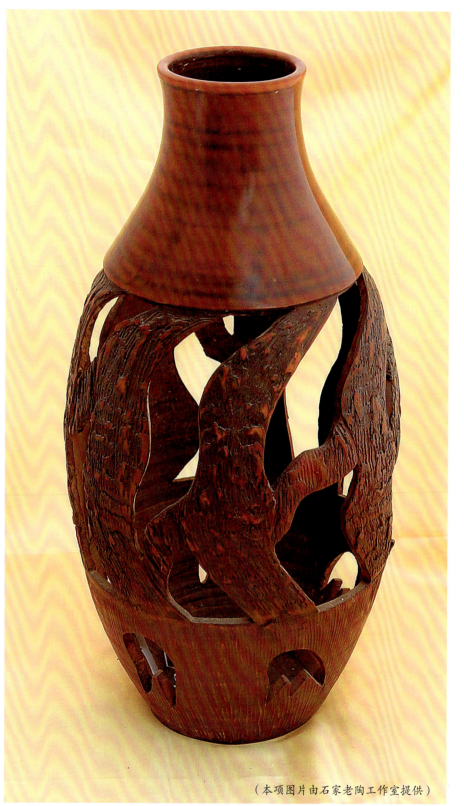

（本项图片由石家老陶工作室提供）

龙山黑陶制作技艺

龙山黑陶制作技艺

 Longshan Black Pottery

拉坯

雕刻

闷烧

　　黑陶出现于龙山文化时期的章丘区域，之后制作工艺消失了数千年，1980年重新烧制成功，现为市级非遗项目。龙山黑陶的烧制，要经过选土、制泥、制坯、刻花、烧制、封窑、出窑等若干工序。其中以传统工艺制作的蛋壳陶，技术难度高，以其"黑如漆、亮如镜、薄如纸、声如磬"而天下闻名。过去龙山黑陶多以仿制古代器皿为主，现在转为以创作为主、仿制为辅。

Craftsmanship of black pottery came into being during the Longshan Culture period in Zhangqiu region. After it disappeared for thousands of years, skillful craftsmen succeeded in firing black pottery in 1980, which is one of the city-level intangible cultural heritage projects today. To kiln black pottery, the firing process consists of preparing clay, jiggering, engraving, firing, sealing up and sealing off. Among all kinds of black potteries, eggshell pottery, which is much more exquisite and much more technically difficult than any others, is well-known throughout the world. Its color is as black as ebony and bright as a mirror. Its thickness is as thin as paper. Given a tap on it, it sounds like a chime. In the past craftsmen made imitations of ancient utensils; however, they focus more on innovation of black potteries today.

清洗

黑陶挂釉瓶

传承人刘德功在介绍黑陶文化

商河老粗布制作技艺

商河纺织老粗布已有1000多年的历史，明、清、民国时期遍及全县，现为市级非遗项目。商河老粗布用木制的纺车纺线、织机编织，经过选棉花、轧棉花、搓布绩、纺线、染线、络线、牵机、织布、修整等十几道工序，有翻花、雪花、雏鸡花、野鸡花等十几种花样，现已发展到各种成品。商河老粗布柔软舒适、古朴典雅，越来越与人们返璞归真的需求相契合。

In Shanghe County, local industrious women have been weaving the traditional coarse cloth since 1000 years ago. As one of the city-level intangible cultural heritage projects today, the art of weaving covered all the county from different periods, including the Ming Dynasty, the Qing Dynasty and the period of the Republic of China (1912~1949). Their spinning wheels and weaving machines are made of wood. The traditional process to weave the cloth consists of preparing cotton, spinning thread, dyeing thread, winding thread, weaving and trimming cloth. The patterns, such as snowflakes, coxcombs are primitive, succinct and lively. With a variety of flower patterns, the traditional coarse cloth has developed into different products that satisfy people's needs for the enjoyment of nature.

络线

牵机

织 布

修 整

成 品

黄家烤肉制作技艺

黄家烤肉制作技艺

The Craft of Huangjia Roast Pork

传承人黄伍忠在整理烤肉

花 肉

搓 料

烧 炉

烤 制

出 炉

　　黄家烤肉据说是明朝末年由章丘黄家湾一姓黄的农家所创制，现为市级非遗项目。其制作工艺精细讲究，分为选猪、配料、剔骨、花肉、搓料、腌猪、贴纸、烤肉等步骤，对焖烤的时间以及火候的掌握有很高的要求。其烤肉以皮香酥、肉软嫩，肥而不腻、回味悠长的独特口味为人们所喜爱。

It is said this local-style roast was roasted by a peasant, whose family name's Huang in huangjiawan village in the late Ming Dynasty. Huangjia roast pork is one of the city-level intangible cultural heritage projects. It is specially roasted that includes several steps: selecting swine, deboning swine, rubbing ingredients, salting meat, covering paper and roasting meat. It is important to control roast time and heat. Not only Huangjia roast pork brings gourmets the special flavor and aroma, but its crispy surface and tender meat leaves them with an endless aftertaste.

糖酥烧饼制作技艺

糖酥烧饼制作技艺

The Craft of Sugar Flaky Pastry

采剂儿

包馅

制饼

烤制

成 品

龙桑寺糖酥烧饼是商河县传统名吃，已有100多年的历史，现为市级非遗项目。主要以面粉、食油、糖作原料，先将面粉用油炒煎，取出加香油和调料制成酥。把和好的面擀成饼并抹上酥，制成多层皮并包上糖馅，压制成饼放在炉上烘烤，至两面焦黄即可。主要特点是酥、香、软、脆，甜度适中，味道鲜美。

Sugar flaky pastry, as the famous local traditional snack, has a history of more than 100 years in Longsangsi Town. It is one of the city-level intangible cultural heritage projects today. It is mainly made from flour cooking oil and sugar. First of all, fry the flour with cooking oil and then mix it with sesame oil and flavoring. Next roll the dough into a pastry with the mixture mentioned above. The pastry traditionally has a sweet filling of peanut candy or walnut meat. Lastly, put the pastry in the oven until it turns brown on both sides. Take a bite—it tastes crispy, tender and delicious.

包 装

齐毛笔制作技艺

齐毛笔制作技艺

The Craft of Chinese Brush in Jinan

传承人于春明在给笔杆刮膛

挑乳子

砌材子

采狼尾

装笔头

修 笔

成 品

齐笔源于春秋战国时的齐国，后来传入北方各省，明清时期在济南发展较快，现为市级非遗项目。齐笔与湖笔、宣笔同样历史悠久，但工艺自成一派，现主要生产狼须毫、羊鼠须毫等高级毛笔。生产过程分为做笔头（水盆）和修笔（干作）两个环节，需经过扒毛、挑乳子、砌材子、垫笔、梳贴子、圆头、覆毛、结头、配杆、刮膛、修笔、上菜、刻字等几十道工序完成。

As its name suggests, the craft of Qi brush originated from the State of Qi (now known as Shandong Peninsula) during the Spring and Autumn Period, which spread to northern provinces later and developed fast in Jinan during the Ming and Qing Dynasty. Now the craft is one of the city-level intangible cultural heritage projects. Qi brush, as well as Hu brush and Xuan brush has a long history in China, while Qi preserve its own style. Its top-grade Chinese brush is the brush made of weasel's hair (or cane rat's hair). Its main process is divided into two phases: making the tip of the brush (with water), decorating the brush (without water). It can only be finished through more than ten steps, including picking and cleaning hair, pressing and twisting hair, fixing the tip to the grip and carving characters and so on.

明式柴木家具制作技艺

明式柴木家具制作技艺

The Craft of Ming-style Furniture of Hardwood

传承人徐光祥在打磨家具

明洪武年间，山西移民将其家具制作技艺与济南本地技艺相结合，产生了济南明式柴木家具，现为市级非遗项目。历城区董家镇一带的柴木家具多选用楸木、榆木、核桃木等本地优良木材，按明代样式和工艺制作，分为桌案类、椅凳类、台架类等几类。明式柴木家具造型朴素自然，卯榫严实不露，瘿木装饰独特，色泽温润舒适，极具审美情趣。

Some people left Shanxi Province for Jinan and brought in their craft of wooden furniture during the Ming Dynasty. The craft of Ming-style furniture of hardwood, which is one of the city-level intangible cultural heritage projects today, embodies the combination of the outside and the local craft. Most of the local furniture is made of elm, walnut, and catalpa wood in Dongjia Town of Licheng District. The furniture is divided into three types: desks, chairs and cupboards. Ming-style furniture has kept folk art style and handicraft of the Ming Dynasty. As you see, each piece of furniture embodies simple but exquisite design, plain but unique styles, natural but cozy colors.

靠背长椅和茶几

八仙桌、太师椅和条几

交椅

玫瑰椅

梯形橱

玉谦旗袍制作技艺

玉谦旗袍制作技艺

The Craft of Yuqian Cheongsam

济南玉谦旗袍店创始于清同治年间，其旗袍制作随历史演变而发展，现为市级非遗项目。玉谦旗袍的制作，秉承镶边、滚边、嵌边、盘扣、贴花、绣花、手绘等传统旗袍制作工艺，又将欧式晚礼服的设计运用到旗袍设计中，第五代继承人于仁谦又解决了用真丝烂花绒和真丝立绒制作旗袍的技术难题，制作出的旗袍格调高雅、款式新颖，深受各界好评。

Yuqian Cheongsam Shop originated in Jinan during the reign of Emperor Tongzhi of the Qing Dynasty. As one of the city-level intangible cultural heritage projects, it has been developing along with the historical development. To make up a perfect cheongsam, the craftsman needs the traditional tailoring and sewing technology. In more specific terms, the processes include sewing a piece of material to the edge of the fabric, stitching the traditional knotted Chinese buttons, doing embroidery on the cheongsam. The technical difficulties of burnt-out velvet and silk upright pile have been solved by the fifth generation of Yuqian's heirs. Yuqian's cheongsams combine delicately the classic elegant style and the design elements of modern European-style evening dress with the pure and elegant color, and the elegance of Chinese characteristics, which are praised by all walks of life.

传承人于仁谦在剪裁

设计

熨烫

样衣

柜台

崮山馍馍制作技艺

崮山馍馍制作技艺

The Craft of Gushan Steamed Bun

崮山馍馍产自长清区大崮山村，始创于明末，曾为皇家贡品，现为市级非遗项目。崮山馍馍选用唐王寨下800亩良田生产的小麦磨面，用酒曲发酵，不使用发酵粉，无任何添加剂，经过人工和面、压面、揉馍、排馍、上锅、起锅、点梅花等18道工序加工而成。馍馍10个一排，一面焦黄，既可冷食，也可热吃，清香甜美，柔中间韧。

As the tribute for the royal courts, created in the late Ming Dynasty, Gushan steamed bun, which is one of the city-level intangible cultural heritage projects, comes from Dagushan Village of Changqing District. Derived from the wheat of local fertile land in Tangwangzhai, the flour is brewed with distiller's yeast without baking powder and other food additives. Its making process requires eighteen steps, including kneading dough, pressing dough, making buns, steaming buns and stamping the patterns of plum blossom on steamed buns. As you see, ten steamed buns are in a row on the tray. Each steamed bun has one brown side. Heated or not, it tastes sweet and chewy.

酒曲发酵

手工採剂儿

人工杠压

贴馍馍

出锅

点梅花

傳统戏剧

「传统戏剧」 Traditional Classical Theatre

济南吕剧

　　济南吕剧原名"坐腔扬琴"、"化妆扬琴"，发源于200多年前的山东琴书与花鼓灯、小曲、拖腔等的结合，现为国家级非遗项目。1951年正式成立山东省第一个吕剧专业剧团——济南鲁声琴剧团，1953年定名为济南市吕剧团。济南吕剧主要由"四平"、"二板"及部分曲牌构成，曲调简单朴实、优美动听、易学易唱，主要流传于山东中西部和北部，为广大群众所喜爱。

Lü Opera, whose original name is sitting down and singing to the accompaniment of dulcimer or performing in costume to the accompaniment of dulcimer, rose from the comprehensive art forms over 200 years ago, including Shandong Qinshu (local story-telling mainly in song with musical accompaniment) , Huagudeng(a kind of folk dance form originated from Huai River Basin), Xiaoqu(folk popular songs) and Denqiang(the intonation with pause and transition in rhythm). Today, Lü Opera is one of the state-level intangible cultural heritage projects. Found in 1951, Jinan Lusheng Theatrical Troupe was the first professional troupe of Lü Opera in Shangdong Province, which was renamed Jinan Lü Opera Troupe.The tune-patterns consist of siping tune (the basic tune, deriving from folk song style of Fengyang Song) , erban tune (the main tune, featuring in changes of rhythm) and other tune-patterns. Since its tunes are simple and pure, pleasant to the ears and easy to learn, Lü Opera, which spreads mainly in the middle, western and northern regions of Shandong Province, is popular among the people.

济南皮影

The Shadow Puppetry in Jinan

起源于汉代的皮影戏自1917年传入济南，不仅流传于山东，同时影响到河北、河南、安徽等地，现为国家级非遗项目。济南皮影戏银幕比较宽大，人物线条粗犷，造型写意夸张，花纹接近民间剪纸，银幕显像清晰生动。由一人或多人操作，配以音乐和唱腔。唱腔吸收了西河调、山东琴书、河南坠子中的部分曲调，念白用济南方言。

Originated in the Han Dynasty, the shadow puppet play, also called "shadow play", was introduced in Jinan in 1917, while it widely spread in Hebei Province, Henan Province and Anhui Province in China, with different styles of shadow puppet play in different places. Now it is one of the state-level intangible cultural heritage projects. The followings are distinguishing features of the shadow puppet play in Jinan. The stage for shadow puppet is a fairly broad white cloth screen. Most of the faces of shadow figures are depicted in thick profile. Representing as they do human or animals, the faces of the shadow figures are exaggerated. The shadow puppet looks similar to a paper cut. The screen often takes on a clear and vivid scene. One player or more than one hold the human figures which can sing and dance controlled by the players. Usually, there are several performing artists showing the folk music and Chinese traditional operas for the audience, such as Xihe Tune (story-telling mainly in song with musical accompaniment, especially a drum, also called "Xihe drum"), Shandong Qinshu, Henan zhuizi (local story-telling mainly in song with musical accompaniment). It is common to use Jinan dialect in their musical dialogues.

国家级非遗代表性传承人李兴时在制作皮影偶人

济南京剧

济南京剧

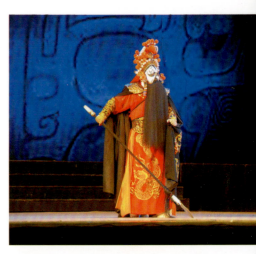

清光绪元年（1875年）济南已有京班雏形，解放后成立"大众京剧团"，现为省级非遗项目。济南号称京剧大码头，光绪年间就有"高升班"和"如意班"，金少山、余叔岩、梅兰芳、李万春、程砚秋、尚小云、荀慧生、马连良、谭福英、奚啸伯等京剧大家都曾在济南演出。进入新世纪后，济南京剧院创编排演了新型京剧《凤游城》、《长剑歌》、《李清照》、《重瞳项羽》等剧目，多次在国家级赛事上获奖。

In 1875, there was an embryonic form of troupe of Beijing Opera in Jinan. After the People's Republic of China was founded, Dazhong Beijing Opera Troupe was established in Jinan, which is one of the province-level intangible cultural heritage projects today. Jinan has been known by reputation as "a big dock of Beijing Opera". There was Gaosheng Troupe and Ruyi Troupe during the reign of Emperor Guangxu of the Qing Dynasty in Jinan. Beijing Opera Masters, just like Jin Shaoshan, Yu Shuyan, Mei Lanfang, Li Wanchun, Cheng Yanqiu, Shang Xiaoyun, Xun Huisheng, Ma Lianliang, Tan Fuying and Xi Xiaobo, appeared on the stage in Jinan. In the new century, Jinan Beijing Opera Troupe has created and performed some new plays, including "Lady Godiva" (adapted from a legend story, originated from Coventry, the UK, about a heroine saving the people from the disaster), "Changjian' ge" (a new historical Beijing Opera), "Li Qingzhao" (a Chinese female writer and poet of the Song Dynasty), "Double-pupil Xiang Yu" (a Chinese historic hero). By virtue of these plays, the troupe performers have won many national awards.

王皮戏

Wang Pi Play

王皮戏也称"王皮调"，清道光年间传入平阴县孔村镇郭柳沟村，现为省级非遗项目。现仅存《十八大姐逗王皮》一个剧目，讲述王皮匠带18个老婆观灯产生的种种矛盾，讽刺旧社会一夫多妻的婚姻制度。开演前先以舞蹈"跑灯"为开场，正戏唱腔以"耍孩儿"、"叠断桥"、"桂枝香"等明、清曲牌为主，舞蹈场图复杂、结构严谨，戏剧曲调流畅、委婉绮丽。

Introduced into Guoliugou Village in Kongcun Town of Pingyin County, during the reign of Emperor Daoguang of the Qing Dynasty, Wang Pi Play is also called "Wang Pi Tune", which is one of the province-level intangible cultural heritage projects. Nowadays, the only existing play about Wang Pi is "Wives Tease Wang Pi". Wang Pi, which was not a true name, in fact, his name's Wang Qingchun, who was a shoemaker. Occasionally he got eighteen handicapped wives from a shelter. After some time, contradictions couldn't be avoided between Wang and his wives. Wives Tease Wang Pi just tells us that Wang with his wives watched festive lanterns in the streets then they had all their problems—the irony of all this is polygamy of the old society. Before the beginning of the play, all the actors held different kinds of lanterns running to the performing place. And then they danced around the performing place with changes of formation. When the play started, the actors sang and danced in the local dialect and distinctive costume. With the complicated choreography, the perfect story structure and the fluent, beautiful tunes, the whole play is loved by the masses.

（本项图片由平阴县文化局提供）

五音戏

Wuyin Play

五音戏也称"肘鼓子戏"（或"周姑子"），清康熙年间起源于章丘市文祖镇青野村一带，流传于鲁中多地，现为省级非遗项目。五音戏是集唱、舞、乐于一体的发展较为完善的戏剧曲种，可演几人小戏和十几人的连本剧，角色分为生、旦、净、丑各行，旋律从秧歌调中脱胎而来，唱词、念白用当地方言，服饰、道具、脸谱等类似京剧，乐器以锣鼓加弦乐为主。

Dating from Qingye Village in Wenzu Town of Zhangqiu City during the reign of Emperor Kangxi of the Qing Dynasty, and then spreading in the middle region of Shandong Province, Wuyin Play is one of the province-level intangible cultural heritage projects now. The roles of Wuyin Play are divided into four categories, including sheng (male roles), dan (female roles), jing (painted face) and chou (clowns). The melody is derived from yangko (a popular rural folk dance), singing in local dialect. Its division of roles and its performance style are similar to Beijing Opera. The music comes from the sonorous sound of Chinese traditional instruments, such as stringed instruments, gongs and drums.

平陰木偶戲

平阴木偶戏

Pingyin Puppet Show

平阴木偶戏于清康熙年间由外地传入平阴，影响范围曾广及天津、聊城、泰安、济宁、开封等地，现为市级非遗项目。平阴木偶戏属于北方"杖头木偶"，是一种融汇了雕刻、化妆、表演、音乐、舞美诸元素的民间戏曲艺术。表演者隐藏于布幔下用木棍举着偶人表演，演员以"山东梆子"为曲调边唱边操作，主要演出《铡美案》、《大辕门》、《天仙配》等历史传统剧目。

Introduced to Pingyin County of Jinan, the puppet show is one of the city-level intangible cultural heritage projects today, which dates back to the reign of Emperor Kangxi of the Qing Dynasty, influencing other regions, including Tianjin, Liaocheng, Taian, Jining and Kaifeng. Through the technique of carving, making up and performing, a puppet show combines the beauty of traditional Chinese opera art and the characteristics of the rod puppet show. Behind a cloth wall, the operators play puppets, which are controlled by a stick attached to the puppet's main body parts. The puppet show is a drama form in which the player holds the human figures, singing and dancing in tune of Shandong Bangzi Opera, to the gong and drum music, playing a series of stories, such as "The Case of Chen Shimei" (it is a historical opera in which Chen Shimei, who abandoned his wife and son, was finally guillotined), "Father wants to kill Son at the Gate of a Government Office" (one of Chinese traditional historical operas) and "The Heavenly Maid and the Mortal" (Chinese traditional love story) and so on.

（本项图片由平阴县文化局提供）

章丘梆子

章丘梆子

Zhangqiu Bangzi

　　章丘梆子源于山西蒲州梆子和陕西秦腔，于明末清初传入，与章丘本地语言、秧歌、民间音乐相融而成，现为市级非遗项目。章丘梆子也称"东路梆子"、"山东吼"，演员的行头、脸谱及唱、念、做、打等表演形式与京剧大体相同，唱腔有板腔和曲牌两种，演唱高亢明亮、尾音上挑。较有影响的剧目有：《赵匡胤下河东》、《双锁山》、《破洪州》、《宝剑记》等。

Zhangqiu Bangzi is derived from Shanxi Bangzi and Qingqiang operas, which were introduced to Jinan during the late Ming and early Qing dynasties, singing in local dialect, dancing in yangko style. Zhangqiu Bangzi is one of the city-level intangible cultural heritage projects today, which is also called "Donglu Bangzi" or "Shangdong Hou". Its division of roles and its performance style are similar to Beijing Opera. The actor with whiskers plays the leading male role and his singing style is forceful and solemn. The actress displays loud and clear singing. The well-known Zhangqiu Bangzi includes "Emperor Zhao Kuangyin with his army assaults the Northern Han Dynasty", "Shuangsuo Mountain" (a historical opera about warfare and romantic love), "Break Through Hongzhou" (The Heroine of the Yangs) and "A Sword Story" (a historical opera based on Outlaws of the Marsh) and so on.

柳子戏

Liuzi Opera

柳子戏又称"弦子戏"，流行于山东、河南、安徽、江苏、河北部分地区，平阴县任庄柳子戏班初建于明万历年间，现为市级非遗项目。平阴柳子戏兴盛时演出40多个剧目，主要曲牌有《锁南枝》、《黄莺儿》、《驻云飞》、《画眉序》等，唱腔由众多不同宫调、板式的曲牌构成，舞台语言以当地方言为主，伴奏乐器以曲笛、笙、小三弦为主，典雅古朴、多姿多彩。

Liuzi Opera is also called Chord Opera which is popular in such regions as Shandong, Henan, Anhui, Jiangsu, Hebei and so on. The theatrical troupe, which is now a municipal non-cultural heritage project, was originally set up in Ren Village, Pingyin County. There were over 40 plays when Pinyin Liuzi Opera was in booming period. It's main tunes consist of Lock the South Branch, Huang Yinger, Zhuyun Fei, Hua Mei and so on. Its arias include plays which vary in modes and plate types. Its stage language is mainly the local language. Its accompanied musical instruments include whistle, flute and small Sanxian, which are elegant, ancient and colorful.

（本项图片由平阴县文化局提供）

「传统体育」 Traditional Martial Arts

济南形意拳

济南形意拳

Xingyi Boxing

省级非遗代表性传承人杨遵利在练拳

长枪

合影

晨练

形意拳据传源于宋代岳飞，明末清初称"心意六合拳"，清中期定名"形意拳"，上世纪30年代传入济南，现为省级非遗项目。济南形意拳属于内家拳，有拳法练习和器械练习，以阴阳五行学说为基础，将拳理、道理、医理贯通一体，神形并重、内外兼修，动作稳捷扎实、舒展明快、严密紧凑，努力使习练者思想得以升华、技能得以悟化、身心得以健康。

According to the legend, Xingyi Boxing was originated from Yue Fei, in the Song Dynasty. It was called "Xinyiliuhe Boxing" and was denominated Xingyi Boxing in the mid-term of the Qing Dynasty. It was introduced to Jinan in the 1930s, which is a provincial non-cultural heritage project. Jinan Xingyi Boxing belongs to internal fist, which includes boxing practice and apparatus practice. It's based on the Theory of Yin, Yang and Five Elements, and combines the boxing theory with the morality and the medical knowledge. It attaches equal importance to body and spirit, and is internal and external. It has the stable and solid actions, the bright stretch, and is tight and compact. It enables the practicers to sublimate their spirits, comprehend their skills, and keep their physical and mental health.

双人棍术对练

谭氏摔跤

谭氏摔跤

Tanshi Wrestling

抢 手

抖皮条大摆桩

踢 儿

勾 子

谭氏摔跤在济南已有100多年的历史，过去曾开跤场以卖艺谋生，现为市级非遗项目。谭式摔跤属中国式摔跤，在全国"四大跤城"之一的济南享有盛名。其动作干脆利落、优美大方，对抗性、观赏性极强，自创的"谭氏勾子"分为单撒手反挂门勾子和散手勾子，被誉为"神勾子"。

Tanshi Wrestling has a long history of 100 years in Jinan, which used to make a living by opening the wrestling area to perform its skills, and now is a municipal non-cultural heritage project. Tanshi Wrestling belongs to Chinese Wrestling, and enjoys a good reputation in Jinan which is regarded as one of the great four wrestling cities. The action of Tanshi Wrestling is flat and neat, elegant and decent, and it has the wonderful opposability and appreciation. Self-created "Tanshi Hook", which is honored with "Magical Hook", is divided into Dan San Shou Fan Gua Men Hook and San Shou Hook.

传承人谭强（右）在走式子

翻挂门勾子

武当济南太乙门

武当济南太乙门

传承人林树基在带领学员练拳

玄门剑

五虎枪

剑术

金刚拳

双龙钩

　　武当太乙门是道家武术的一个门派，民国初年在济南开始传播并传承至今，现为市级非遗项目。济南太乙门包括拳术、器械、对练、实战技法、养生功法、硬功功法等内容，有醉猴拳、埋伏拳、金刚拳、玄门剑、缠丝刀、五虎枪、金刚棍、峨眉刺、金刚圈等拳法和器械套路。是一种集技击、养生、内功和文化为一体，将习武、养生、益智、医疗相融合的传统文化体系。

Wudang Tai Yi School is a school of Taoist Martial Arts, which is now a municipal non-cultural heritage project, has been spread in Jinan since the early Republic of China (1912-1949). Jinan Tai Yi School includes boxing, apparatus, pair exercise, actual combat skills, Qigong Practice, and toughening exercise. It contains Zuihou Boxing, Maifu Boxing, Jingang Boxing, Xuanmen Sword, Chansi Knife, Wuhu Gun, Jingang Stick, Ermei Thorn, Jigang Circle and so on. It connects martial arts with Qigong Practice, inner strength and culture. It is a cultural system which combines martial arts with Qigong Practice, intelligence and medical treatment.

太平拳

太平拳

　　太平拳在清康熙年间由王翀宇创立，发源于平阴县孔村镇，流传于安徽、浙江、山西及东北部分地区，现为市级非遗项目。太平拳主要包括基本功法、拳术套路、器械套路、对练套路、实战技术、硬功功法、轻功功法、养生功法等内容，有拳、掌、大刀、大枪、大铲、飞龙剑、射艺等套路，吸收南北武术精华，积累多年实战经验，形成了稳、准、狠的特点。

Taiping Boxing was founded by Wang Chongyu in Kangxi Emperor of the Qing Dynasty. It was originated in Kongsun Town, Pingyin County, and was popular in such regions as Anhui, Zhejiang, Shanxi and north-east areas, which is a municipal non-cultural heritage project. It includes basic Gongfa, a series of boxing, apparatus and pair exercise skills, practical skills, toughening exercise, Qigong Practice and so on. It also has a series of tricks about boxing, palm, broad sword, rifle, shovel, Flying Dragon Sword, shooting and so on. Absorbing the essence of the north-south martial arts and accumulating the practical experience of many years, Taiping Boxing has the characters of steadiness, accuracy and ruthlessness.

传承人王大庆在表演剑术

二指禅

合 影

守门双铜

72斤太平大刀

桩功练习

传统美术

「传统美术」 Traditional Folk Arts

鲁绣

鲁绣

Luxiu Embroidery

省级非遗代表性传承人徐秀玲在创作

鹊华秋色图

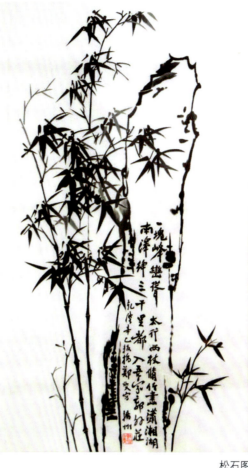

奔马图

献寿图

松石图

羲之行散图

　　鲁绣起源于春秋战国时期，汉代遍及山东，一直传承至今，现为省级非遗项目。鲁绣是北方民间刺绣的代表，图案苍劲、质地坚实、用色鲜明、针法豪放，有散套针、抢针、齐针、打籽等几十种针法。最为突出的是用人发与丝线结合施绣的发丝绣，擅长表现中国画和书法作品，还可精绣人物肖像和油画，堪称中国刺绣一绝。

Originated in the Chunqiu and Zhanguo Periods, spreading all over Shandong Province in the Han Dynasty. Luxiu Embroidery is recognized as one of the province-level intangible cultural heritage projects. As representative of northern folk embroider, the pictures of Luxiu Embroidery are vigorous, materials strong, vivid color, embroidery technique bold using tens of embroidery technique, such as emboitement embroidery, rapid embroidery, all directions embroidery and preparing-embroidery. The most impressive is hair and silk embroidery, mixing hair and silk together, which is skillful in showing Chinese drawings and handwritings, as well as portraits and paintings. The hair and silk embroidery is one of the best in Chinese embroidery.

济南面塑

济南面塑

传承人何晓铮在创作

老济南人家

太白醉酒

玉米蝈蝈

济南面塑俗称"捏面人"、"捏糯米人",清代由曹州(今菏泽)传入,曾出国表演展售,至今兴盛不衰,现为省级非遗项目。济南面塑主要以面粉、糯米、蜂蜜、色膏、防腐用品等为原材料,借助拨子、滚钗、切刀、神铎等工具塑造形象。早期创作对象多为戏剧或神话人物,现在题材十分丰富,且色彩鲜明、手法细腻、形象逼真、人物传神。

Jinan dough modeling, called "art work made from powder" in dialect, was introduced in Jinan in the Qing dynasty from Caozhou (known as Heze today). Jinan dough modeling has been shown and sold abroad many times and is still popular today. It is recognized as one of the province-level intangible cultural heritage projects. Jinan dough modeling, is mainly made from powder, sticky rice, honey, color cream, anticorrosive products, with the help of various tools such as plectrum, cutting knife, rolling hairpin and ect. The earlier products were about the people of opera or legend, while at present topics are various, and the colors are bright. Technique is proficient, and the figures are vivid.

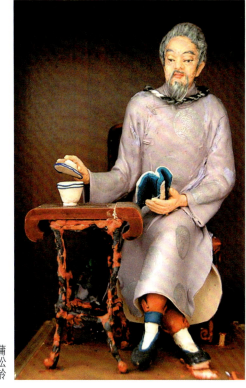

蒲松龄

寿星

四大天王

济南剪纸

济南剪纸

Paper-cut in Jinan

传承人尚玉菊在剪纸

济南剪纸发源时间无法考定，清末民国已有专业作坊批量制作销售，现为市级非遗项目。济南地区民间剪纸主要来自渤海地区和胶东地区，或粗犷豪放，或精巧生动。过去主要以刺绣花样、喜花、顶棚花、窗花、墙花为主，新中国成立后增加了更多的现实主义内容，涉及民间故事、神话传说、现实人物、飞禽走兽等各个方面。作品写实性强，造型严谨，手法细致。

It is unknown when Jinan Paper-cut origins. But at the end of the Qing dynasty, some workshops produced and sold them at a large scale. Now it is one of the city-level intangible cultural heritage projects. Paper-cut in Jinan was introduced from Bohai district and east part of Shandong Province. Some are rough and bold, while some are delicate and vivid. In the past, it was used as decoration for wedding, or sample of embroidery. After the founding of the People's Republic of China, the topics are more realistic, concerning folk stories, legend, real people and so on. The products are the reflection of reality. The style is precise and the technique is meticulous.

龙凤呈祥

梁山泊108将（局部）

辛弃疾

张飞怒打督邮

黑旋风 李逵

李 逵

济南泥塑

济南泥塑

Clay Sculpture in Jinan

传承人陈俊岭作品

搓麻绳

编筐

双簧

包 公

烤火烧

做笤帚

卖蒲窝

济南泥塑可追溯到大汶口、龙山文化时期，灵岩寺宋代彩塑罗汉更被誉为"海内第一名塑"，现为市级非遗项目。济南泥塑一般选用黏而细腻的土，有时加些棉絮、纸或蜂蜜制作。大型泥塑以神像、人像等为主，多经过制子儿、翻模、脱胎、着色四道工序完成；中小型泥塑多以反映现实题材的传说、故事、人物、动物等为主。以造型生动、色彩艳丽而著称。

Jinan Clay Sculpture originated from Dawenkou and Longshan periods. Colored clay arhat sculpture of the Song Dynasty in Lingyan Temple is regarded as "the first sculpture all over the world" and now is one of the city-level intangible cultural heritage projects. Jinan sculpture is made of sticky and smooth clay, mixed with paper, cotton and honey. It is mainly about portraits and has four procedures such as designing, modeling, making bodiless lacquerware and coloring. It is all about legends, stories and animals. It is famous for its vivid sculpt and bright colors.

侯氏社火脸谱

侯氏社火脸谱

Houshi Festive Facial Makeup

侯氏社火脸谱起源于清代中末期，先在历城后在天桥由侯氏一家世代传承，现为市级非遗项目。社火脸谱原是民间举行社火活动时所戴的面具，后来演变成独立的民间艺术。侯氏脸谱以葫芦和木板为主要材料，在其上绘制彩色脸谱，多以"秦叔宝"、"石敢当"、"钟馗"、"关公"和十二生肖为内容。其造型别致、色彩绚丽，多悬挂于家中借以祛病辟邪。

Festive Facial Makeup of Hou family originated from the middle and the end of the Qing Dynasty. It was passed from generation to generation in Hou family first in Licheng District and later in Tianqiao District. Now it is recognized as the city-level intangible cultural heritage. It used to be masks worn in festive activities and later has become a separate folk art. It is made of wood sheet and calabash, decorated with various makeup, such as "Qin Shubao", "Shi Gandang", "Zhong Kui", "Guan Gong" and Chinese Zodiac. It has vivid sculpt and bright colors. It is usually hung in rooms to avoid bad luck.

传承人侯志新在创作

关公

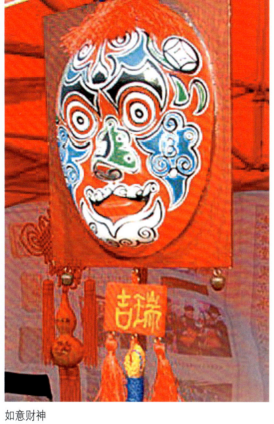

如意财神

脸谱展销

新旧脸谱

脸谱展览

葫蘆雕刻

葫芦雕刻

Bottle Gourd Carving

传承人张冰在刻葫芦

济南葫芦雕刻兴盛于清末到民国时期，上世纪80年代重又兴起，现为市级非遗项目。济南葫芦雕刻是在天然葫芦上用刀进行雕刻的一种手工艺术，包括镂雕、浮雕、刻线、刻面、组合等方式，尤以镂雕为主要特点，体现出朴实自然、玲珑剔透的艺术特征。镂雕的内容主要有福禄寿文字、几何图案和飞虫人物等，浮雕主要表现传说人物及动物、植物。

Bottle Gourd Carving in Jinan thrived at the end of the Qing Dynasty and the Republic of China (1912-1949). From the 1980s, it has become popular and now is recognized as the city-level intangible cultural heritage. It is art carved in natural bottle gourd with knife including enchasing, embossment, scratch and so on. It is specialized in enchasing, naturally and exquisitely. Its topics are mainly about words of happiness, geometric patterns and flying insects as well as portraits. Embossment mainly describes legendary characters, animals and plants.

千福葫芦

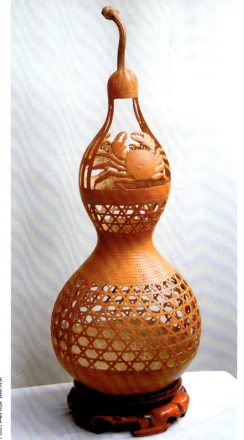

镂雕螃蟹葫芦

百寿葫芦

四君子灯

水浒一百零八将

周氏兔子王

周氏兔子王

Zhoushi Rabbit King

传承人周秉生在创作

单坐虎　　男女兔子王

济南兔子王于清末民初即在济南流行，周氏兔子王制作已传承四代，现为市级非遗项目。济南兔子王原是中秋祭拜月神时与月饼摆在一起供奉的泥制偶像，用黄河细胶泥制胎，施以彩绘，牵以丝线，兔子手中之物可动，是济南独有的泥塑工艺品。周氏兔子王有坐王、站王、兔奶奶、兔子山、大红袍、坐虎、坐墩、坐元宝等十几个品种，尺寸由十几厘米到八十厘米不等。

Zhoushi Rabbit King was popular at the end of the Qing Dynasty and the beginning of the Republic of China (1912-1949). The skills of making rabbit kings have been passed to the 4th generation in Zhou family, and now it is one of the city-level intangible cultural heritage projects. Rabbit kings used to be a clay idle consecrated together with the Queen of the moon and mooncakes. Rabbit kings are made of clay of the Yellow River, decorated with colors and equipped with thread so that the things in its hand can move. It is one of the special clay crafts. Rabbit kings of Zhou family vary from seated kings, standing kings, rabbit grandma and so on, more than ten types in all. The sizes vary from 10cm to 80cm.

兔子王群像

喜庆群像

传统舞蹈

「传统舞蹈」 Traditional Dances

商河鼓子秧歌

商河鼓子秧歌

Shanghe Drum Yangko Dance

商河鼓子秧歌孕育于宋，形成于明，自清至今兴盛不衰，其起源和发展与当地春节民间祭祀有关，现为国家级非遗项目。原表演集歌、舞、丑为一体，舞者自始至终都在不停跑动，故亦称"跑秧歌"。现主要由"伞头"、"鼓子"、"棒槌"三种角色表演，偶有丑角参演。"伞头"左手持平顶伞，右手拿牛胯骨，为演出的指挥者；"鼓子"左手握圆形小扁鼓，右手持鼓槌；"棒槌"双手各握一根两端带穗的枣木棒。鼓子秧歌场图丰富多彩，线路变化多样，舞姿健美雄浑，被誉为"汉族民间男性舞蹈的代表"。

As an intangible heritage project at the national level, Shanghe Drum Yangko Dance is conceived in the Song Dynasty, formed in the Ming Dynasty and has been prosperous since the Qing Dynasty, which is closely involved with the folk sacrifice in the Spring Festival. The original performance consists of 3 roles, namely singers, dancers and clowns, with the dancer constantly performing Yangko dance. Now the roles have been changed into the umbrella holder, drummers and club holders, occasionally with clowns in. The umbrella holder is the director, with an umbrella in his left hand and a piece of calf hipbone in his right hand; the drummer has a round and flat drum in the left hand and a drumstick in the right hand; the club holder has a date stick in his each hand. The dance has various formations and routines and is praised as the representative one of the male dances of Han nationality for its vigorousness and firmness.

章丘芯子

章丘芯子

Zhangqiu Xinzi

章丘芯子是一种民间扮玩活动，起源于明朝，流传于章丘各地，现为国家级非遗项目。表演内容多为戏剧情节或神话故事，用以驱邪祈福。分为"桌芯子"、"车芯子"、"转芯子"、"扛芯子"、"单杆芯子"等多种类型。"转芯子"的表演节奏与抬杆颤幅一致，杆上演员随抬杠颤动舞动彩绸，并同时左右或上下旋转。"扛芯子"由一名强壮男演员和一名儿童演员组成，表演时"芯子"与"扛者"随鼓乐的节奏上下舞动。

As an intangible heritage project at the national level, Zhangqiu Xinzi is a folk recreation activity. It dates back to the Ming Dynasty and spreads all over Zhangqiu. The performance is mainly based on some dramatic plots and mysteries to disperse evil spirits and pray for blessings. The mandrels are divided into table-like ones, vehicle-like ones, turning ones, carried-on-the-shoulder ones, single-pole ones and so on. The performance of turning ones keeps pace with the shaking rhythm of the pole, and the performers on the pole swish colorful ribbon and turn left, right and up and down. The performance of carried-on-the-shoulder one is given by a strong actor who is the carrier and a child actor who is the Xinzi. The carrier and the Xinzi dance up and down to the beat of drums.

横竖转芯子

扛芯子（集体）

单杆芯子

单杆芯子（集体）

横转芯子

扛芯子

花鞭鼓舞

花鞭鼓舞

Ribbon Whip Drum Dance

花鞭鼓舞是流传于商河县张坊乡一带的民间艺术，出现于光绪年间，原为乞讨卖艺形式，现为国家级非遗项目。演员身背腰鼓，双手同时挥舞一尺多长的花鞭，以鞭头用牛皮结成的疙瘩敲击腰鼓面，发出清脆响亮的声音。表演时，花鞭似金蛇狂舞，鼓声像战马奔腾，令人眼花缭乱、精神振奋。

As an intangible heritage project at the national level, Ribbon Whip Drum Dance is a form of folk art spreading in Zhangfang Township of Shanghe County. It dates back to the reign of Emperor Guangxu of the Qing Dynasty, as a means to beg. The performers have a waist drum on them and swish a one-foot-long ribbon whip with two hands, beating the drum with the cowhide knob at the end of the whip and making a clear and loud sound. The whip is like a golden snake dancing wildly and the beat of the drum is like war-horses galloping, which often refreshes the audience and dazzles their eyes.

济阳鼓子秧歌

济阳鼓子秧歌

Jiyang Drum Yangko Dance

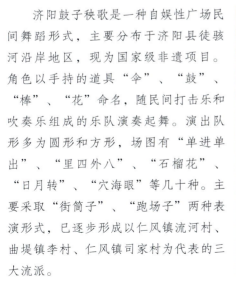

　　济阳鼓子秧歌是一种自娱性广场民间舞蹈形式，主要分布于济阳县徒骇河沿岸地区，现为国家级非遗项目。角色以手持的道具"伞"、"鼓"、"棒"、"花"命名，随民间打击乐和吹奏乐组成的乐队演奏起舞。演出队形多为圆形和方形，场图有"单进单出"、"里四外八"、"石榴花"、"日月转"、"穴海眼"等几十种。主要采取"街筒子"、"跑场子"两种表演形式，已逐步形成以仁风镇流河村、曲堤镇李村、仁风镇司家村为代表的三大流派。

As an intangible heritage project at the national level, Jiyang Drum Yangko Dance, a form of folk recreation dance performed on the square, mainly spreads in the region around the Tuhai River of Jiyang County. The roles of the dance are named after the properties of the umbrella, the drum, the club and the flower. The performers dance to the rhythm of the percussion instruments and wind instruments, in the formation of circle or square, making tens of patterns, such as single person in and out, four inside and eight outside, flower of pomegranate, the movement of the sun and the moon, the eye of the deep sea. The performances are mainly given in the lanes and on the square. Generally, there are three groups, with Liuhe Village in Renfeng County, Li Village in Quti County and Sijia Village in Renfeng County respectively being its representatives.

绣球灯

绣球灯

　　绣球灯于明末清初在长清区赵营村开始出现，是武术和民间艺术结合的一种舞蹈艺术形式，现为省级非遗项目。表演由一个（或其偶数）持手龙的演员和数个（或其倍数）持绣球的演员进行，有"龙珠显威"、"群龙戏水"、"麦浪翻滚"、"螺师结顶"、"瓦步晃珠"等24种阵型，气势磅礴、粗犷豪放、动作舒展、阵型多变。手龙由竹篾编成外裹彩绸，龙身有手柄，龙体内有喷火装置；绣球灯由竹条扎成外裹红绸，内置灯光，可转动。

As an intangible heritage project at the provincial level, Silk Ball Lamp first appeared in Zhaoying Village in Changqing District, which is a combination of Kung fu and folk art. The performance is given by one or two persons with a dragon in hand and several persons with silk balls in hand, and consists of 24 dance formations, such as the dragon pearl shining, dragons playing with water, wheat waves rolling, pearl groups on the head, small paces with balls rolling and so on. The performance is powerful and magnificent with various formations and easy-going movement. The hand-held dragon and the silk ball lamp are woven of bamboo skin covered with red silk, with a handle on the dragon body and a fire gadget inside. The silk ball lamp, equipped with light inside, is movable.

梆鼓秧歌

Bang Drum Yangko Dance

梆鼓秧歌据传是清乾隆年间以做、卖豆腐为基本场景创造出的一种舞蹈，至上世纪30年代失传，90年代经挖掘整理重新演出，现为省级非遗项目。梆鼓秧歌主要以梆、包、鼓为道具、分角色，由12、24、36或48人表演，以十几种不同的步法、手法、身法，配以梆鼓的打击声和背景音乐，演变出"豆腐架"、"小推磨"、"串磨坊"、"走街串巷"等场图，表现做、卖豆腐的劳动场景和欢快热烈的气氛。

As an intangible heritage project at the provincial level, Bang Drum Yangko Dance is said to have dated from the reign of Emperor Qianlong of the Qing Dynasty, which failed to be handed down in the 1930s and resumed in the 1990s after being exploited and sorted. The performance is given by 12, 24, 36 or 48 people, with the properties of rattles, bags and drums which are played by different roles. The performance has tens of gaits, hand movements and bodily movements accompanied by the beat of rattle and drum and background music, which can convey clear pictures of tofu stand, turning a quern, visiting grain mills, selling tofu through the lanes and so on, which create scenes of making and selling tofu and a lively and hot atmosphere.

加鼓通

加鼓通

加鼓通亦称"打长板"，源于古代祈雨活动，定型于明末，现在是一种春节民间舞蹈，流传于平阴县境，现为省级非遗项目。表演时三人一组，其中"引子"（县官）一人，两串铜铃十字披挂；"腿子"（随从）两人，手持竹制夹板，三人相互呼应，随"加鼓通、加鼓通，加鼓、加鼓、加鼓通"的节奏起舞，演出粗犷热烈、滑稽乖巧、幽默风趣。

Jiagutong is also called playing long plate, originated from the praying-for-rain activity in the ancient and having the fixed pattern at the end of the Ming Dynasty. Now it is a form of folk dance performed in the Spring Festival, spreading in Pingyin County, which is an intangible heritage project at the provincial level. The performing group consists of three people, including a county magistrate with two clusters of bronze bells crossed, and two servants with bamboo plywood. The three persons interact well, dancing to the rhythm of Jianggutong, Jiagutong and Jiagu, Jiagu, Jiagutong, whose performance is boorish, enthusiastic, amusing, cute and humorous.

高跷（高家）

高跷（乔家）

Stilt-walking (Qiaojia)

　　济阳县乔家高跷已有100多年的历史，是百姓为欢庆丰收或节日而表演的一种民间舞蹈，现为市级非遗项目。乔家高跷以《西游记》、《白蛇传》等人物作扮相，主要有"二虎把门"、"月子花"、"十字街"、"四里八外"、"剪丁股"、"上木板"等套路，融舞蹈、音乐、杂技于一体，动作惊险洒脱，场面热烈欢快，形式灵活多样，服装斑斓多彩。

As an intangible heritage project at the municipal level, Qiaojia Stilt-walking of Jiyang County has a history of over 100 years, which is a form of folk dance to celebrate harvests and festivals. The performers are dressed up as the characters in Pilgrimage to the West and the Tale of the White Serpent, and the performance routine consists of Two Tigers on the Door, Moon-shaped Flowers, Crossroads, Four Inside and Eight Outside, Jian Dinggu, ON the Board and so on, which combines dance, music and acrobatics. The performance with flexible and various patterns and colorful costumes is breathtaking and free and easy, creating a hot, lively and cheerful atmosphere.

济南西关高跷秧歌

济南西关高跷秧歌

Xiguan Stilt Yangko Dance of Jinan

　　明朝中期西关高跷秧歌自鲁西南传入济南，至今已有600年历史，现为市级非遗项目。表演时的行进队形为"船形灯"状，两头高中间低，形成文、武高，傻小子、丑妞矮的格局。开场后集体亮相走圈，然后演出打棒、青蛇白蛇戏老艄公等节目，最后以叠罗汉谢场。以其奇特、惊险的特点赢得观众。

As an intangible heritage at the municipal level, Xiguan Stilt Yangko Dance of Jinan has a history of over 600 years, introduced into Jinan from the southwest Shandong Province in the middle period of the Ming Dynasty. The progressive performance formation is like a boat-shaped lamp, with the two tips higher and the centre lower and forming a formation of taller military and literary gifts and shorter silly lads and homely girls. The performance begins with circling around the performing field, includes stick beating, The Legend of Green Snake and White Snake, Old Helmsman and so on, and ends with pyramid building. The performance which is spectacular and breathtaking attracts a lot of audience.

董家伞棍鼓舞

董家伞棍鼓舞

Dongjia Drum Dance with Umbrella and Baton

　　济阳县垛石镇董家村伞棍鼓舞起源于南宋，表演阵型源于演兵阵法，现为市级非遗项目。主要由手持伞和棍的演员在场上表演，锣鼓在场下伴奏。伞头手持红伞带动队伍做各种阵型变化，花棍演员手持两根花棍相互敲打上下翻飞，展现了人们庆祝丰收和节日时的欢快心情。表演刚柔相济、变化多端，主要有"八面埋伏"、"阴阳八卦"、"八仙聚首"等多种阵法。

Dongjia Drum Dance with Umbrella and Baton dates back to the Southern Song Dynasty and originates from maneuver formation, which is an intangible heritage project at the municipal level. Persons with umbrellas and batons perform on the stage accompanied by gongs and drums. The head performer with a red umbrella leads the team to change the formation, while the performers have two flower batons beating and flying up and down, which express people's happiness at harvests and festivals. The performance shows both hardness and softness and has a variety of formations, mainly including Ambush in All Directions, Yinyang Eight-diagram Tactics and Eight Immortals Getting Together.

白庄花棍秧歌

白庄花棍秧歌

Baizhuang Flower Baton Yangko Dance

传承人白吉东做示范教练

白庄花棍秧歌因流传于平阴县白庄村而得名，起源于明代，现为市级非遗项目。表演者手持竹制带铃花棍，按一定套路有规律、有节奏地挥舞击打，形成一套跳跃舞打的连续动作。击打时以花棍碰击臂、腿、腰、背、脚心、手掌等部位或地面，两人以上舞蹈时常常互相对敲，队形有"背对背"、"心合心"、"凤穿花"、"五梅花"、"龙吐水"等，花样繁多，气氛热烈。

Baizhuang Flower Baton Yangko Dance gets its name for being popular in Baizhuang Village in Pingyin County. Originating from the Ming Dynasty, now it is an intangible heritage project at the municipal level. The performers hold bamboo flower baton with bells to swing and beat regularly while leaping and dancing. The flower baton lands on the arms, legs, waist, back, arch of the foot, palm and other parts of the body or on the ground. While two persons are performing, they often beat each other, ranking back to back, heart to heart, like phoenix through flowers, plum blossom of five petals and dragon spitting water, which has a variety of formations and creates a hot atmosphere.

（本项图片由平阴县文化局提供）

章丘龙舞

章丘龙舞

Dragon Dance in Zhangqiu

章丘龙舞据说始于明洪武年间，由于人口迁徙自山西传入，陆续遍布章丘境内，现为市级非遗项目。龙舞表演是章丘人民在正月里的一种扮玩活动，集乐、舞于一体，龙珠翻腾，长龙追随，舞随乐动，欢快热烈。主要有"二龙戏珠"、"火龙入海"、"龙降甘露"、"腾云驾雾"、"火龙戏海"等表演套路，有进行式、圆场式两种表演形式。白天舞彩绘的布龙，晚上舞点着的龙灯。

As an intangible heritage project at the municipal level, Zhangqiu Dragon Dance is said to have dated from the term of Hongwu in the Ming Dynasty. It was introduced into Zhangqiu with the migration of population and gradually spread over all areas of Zhangqiu. Now it is an intangible heritage project at the municipal level. Dragon Dance is a folk recreation activity hold in the first month of the lunar year, combining music with dance, with the dragon ball flying and the dragons following. The dragons dance to the music, hotly and delightfully. The routine performance includes Two Dragons Play with a Pearl, Fire Dragons Dive into the Sea, Dragon Brings Rain, Dragons Speed across the Sky, Fire Dragons Play with the Sea and so on. The performances are given sometimes in progressive form and sometimes in a round place, with colorful cloth dragons dancing in the day and lit dragon lantern dancing in the night.

章丘旱船

章丘旱船

Zhangqiu Land Boat Dance

　　章丘旱船始于明代，是一种民间扮玩的舞蹈形式，在章丘境内广泛流传，现为市级非遗项目。章丘旱船分为草船、花船、双旱船三种，以花船为多。用竹子扎制主体，船衣绘水纹、荷花等图案，船篷上挂彩球、排穗等饰物。表演时，表演者随打击乐节奏跑"之字"、"菱形"、"串8字"、"转五花"等套路，上下翻飞，十分热烈喜悦。

As an intangible heritage project at the municipal level, Zhangqiu Land Boat Dance, a form of folk recreation dance, dates from the Ming Dynasty and is popular in Zhangqiu Area. There are three kinds of boats, grass ones, flower ones and double ones, with the flower ones major. The boat is mainly made of bamboo. The outside is carved with pictures of waves, lotus and ect., and the boat awning is decorated with colorful balls and ranges of ears. While performing, the performers dance in the patterns of the Chinese character 之, diamond and the number 8, turning with the boats flying up and down, creating a hot and delightful atmosphere.

「曲 艺」 Qu Yi—Folk Art Performances of Dialect Rap

山東快書

山东快书

Shandong Clapper Ballad

省级非遗代表性传承人赵光臣（于派）在表演

传承人阴军（高派）在表演

山东快书俗称"唱武老二的"，于清道光十九年（1839年）首演，1940年后在山东各根据地开始创作演出以现实生活为内容的故事，1949年正式定名为山东快书，现为省级非遗项目。山东快书以山东方言演出，台风亲切、韵诵紧凑、夸张俏皮、刚劲粗犷。现在已形成三个艺术派别，"高派"、"杨派"以击打铜质鸳鸯板为伴奏，"于派"以击打四叶竹板为伴奏。

Shandong Clapper Ballad is commonly called Chang Wulaoer De. Its first performance was given in 1839（in the reign of Emperor Daoguang in the Qing Dynasty）. Then since 1940, it had been performed in every Shandong base area, whose stories were based on the real life there and in 1949 was officially named Shandong Clapper Ballad. Now, it is an intangible heritage project at the provincial level. Shandong Clapper Ballad is performed in Shandong dialects. Its style is amiable, compact, exaggerating, amusing, vigorous and boorish. There are three different performing groups, the Group of Gao, the Group of Yang, which is accompanied by bronze clappers with two parts, and the Group of Yu, which is accompanied by bamboo clappers with four parts.

传承人苏俊杰（杨派）在表演

山東琴書

山东琴书

国家级非遗代表性传承人姚忠贤（左）与杨珀在演出

山东琴书又称"唱扬琴"、"山东扬琴"等，发源于清雍正年间的曹州府（今菏泽市），1933年正式定名为山东琴书，济南的山东琴书被称为"北路琴书"，现为省级非遗项目。现在演出时，以敲扬琴和操坠琴者为主唱，其他人伴奏坐唱。演唱已经板腔化，以优美挺拔、和缓舒展、朗朗上口、变化多端为特点，在整理改编传统曲目的基础上创编出众多新曲目。

Shandong Qinshu is also called Chang Yangqin or Shandong Yanqin, originated from Caozhou Prefecture during the reign of Emperor Yongzhen in the Qing Dynasty. In 1933, it was officially named Shandong Qinshu, while the one of Jinan is called Beilu Qinshu, which is an intangible heritage project at the provincial level. Those who play Yangqin and Zhuiqin are leading singers while others accompany as well as sing, sitting there. The performance is in the style of Banqiang and equipped with sweetness, gentleness and changeable tunes, which is also easy to sing. Now many new works are added to the traditional ones which have been sorted and adapted.

山東大鼓

山东大鼓

Shandong Dagu

山东大鼓又名"犁铧大鼓"、"梨花大鼓"，明末清初发源于鲁北、冀南一带农村，清同治年间进入济南，清末曾遍布全省甚至进入南京、汉口、重庆、北京及东北各地，上世纪30年代后期衰落，解放后重新兴起，现为省级非遗项目。演唱或刚劲挺拔，或婉转缠绵，旋律起伏大，演唱技巧高，主要演出《响马传》、《三国演义》、《水浒传》、《西厢记》等传统中短篇书目和新创作的小段。

Shandong Dagu is also called Lihua Dagu. It originated in the countryside in the area of North Shandong and South Hebei at the end of the Ming Dynasty and the beginning of the Qing Dynasty, and was introduced in Jinan during the Reign of Emperor Tong Zhi in the Qing Dynasty. At the end of the Qing Dynasty, it was at its full swing, which was popular all over Shandong Province and even was introduced to Nanjing, Hankou, Chongqing, Beijing and Northeast China. It declined in the late 1930s and resumed after 1949. Nowadays it is an intangible heritage project at the provincial level. The vocal performance is sometimes dynamical and vigorous, and sometimes sweet and lingering. Its melody contains a range of changes which call for superb skills. Some constantly performed works are traditional or newly-adapted, such as the Legend of Highwaymen, The Romance of Three Kingdoms, Tales of the Marshes and Romance of the Western Bower.

评词

评词
Pingci

　　山东评词也称评书，在各种说唱艺术中形成最早，明代臻于成熟，现为省级非遗项目。评词以"道之以德"为传统，以编演新书为长项，以说山东话、讲山东事、说山东人为特色，以折扇、醒木、方巾为道具，讲今论古、说事拉理。演出形式简单方便，表演方式因人而异，讲述故事夹评夹议，刻画事物惟妙惟肖，在山东、华北和东北大部分地区流行。

Pingci, also called Pingshu (storytelling) , is the earliest form of folk rap and became ripe in the Ming Dynasty. Now it is an intangible heritage project at the provincial level. Pingci inherits the tradition of telling stories guided by morality, useful at adapting new stories, and tells stories of Shandong events and persons in Shandong dialects, and a folding fan, an attention-catching block and a piece of kerchief are its props. It is a way to talk over the past and present and presents the facts and reason. It is easy to give Pingci Performance, and its styles are different according to different persons. The performers make comments while telling stories and describe things vividly. Pingci is popular in Shandong and most areas of North and Northeast of China.

省级非遗代表性传承人刘延广在表演

（本项图片由刘延广家人提供）

山東相声

山东相声

　　相声于上世纪20年代初期传入济南，后来北京、天津、济南号称相声艺术的三大码头，现为市级非遗项目。山东相声融京津相声"文"、"爆"之长，形成自己"有文有爆、文爆结合"的独特艺术风格，经常演出《夸住宅》、《蛤蟆鼓》、《树没叶》、《黄鹤楼》等节目，侯宝林、张寿臣、马三立、吉坪三、周德山、刘宝瑞、郭全宝等著名相声艺术家都到济南演出过。

Shandong Crosstalk is an intangible heritage project at the municipal level. Crosstalk was introduced into Jinan in the early 1920s, and later Beijing, Tianjin, and Jinan are known as the three docks of the art of crosstalk. Shandong Crosstalk integrates with the wen and bao, which are the strengths of Beijing and Tianjin Crosstalk, and in turn has its own characteristic of being mild as well as hot and a combination of mildness and hotness. The frequently-performed works are as follows: Boasting the houses, Toad Drum, A Tree without leaves, Huanghe Building. Many crosstalk masters such as Hou Baolin, Zhang Shouchen, Ma Sanli, Ji Pingsan, Zhou Deshan, Liu Baorui, Guo Quanbao and so on have ever performed in Jinan.

长清落子

长清落子

Changqing Laozi

　　长清落子也称"莲花落"、"莲花乐"，宋代已在山东流行，流传于济南和周边泰安、潍坊、德州、聊城一带，现为市级非遗项目。演出时，演唱者右手自打铜钹、左手以大竹板击节，使用本地方言半说半唱。主要演唱《杨家将》、《三国演义》、《郭巨埋儿》、《二十四怕》、《农村孝星》等传统和现代段子，内容群众化、演唱口语化、形式多样化、活动地域化。

Changqing Laozi is also called Lianhua Lao or Lianhua Le. Since the Song Dynasty, it has been popular in Shandong Province, especially in Jinan, Tai'an, Weifang, Dezhou and Liaocheng. While performing, the performer plays the copper cymbals with the right hand, beat the bamboo clappers with the left hand as well as rap in the local dialects. The representative works are as follows: The Generals of Three Kingdoms, Guoju Buries His Son to Support His Old Mother, Twenty-four Worries, The Devoted Sons in the Countryside and so on. The works have popular content, oral lines, various designs and regional characteristics.

传承人徐立平在表演

平陰漁鼓

平阴渔鼓

Pingyin Yugu(a percussion instrument made of bamboo)

传承人朱世平在表演

平阴渔鼓也称"渔鼓书"，原是道家唱"道情"的一种方式，后来演变为民间说唱艺术，现为市级非遗项目。平阴渔鼓由一人持简板抱渔鼓击打说唱，一般有四句"开场白"，接着进入说书的正文。唱腔苍凉豪放，内容通俗易懂，表演充满激情。过去主要表演《金鞭记》、《刘公案》、《岳飞传》等，现在主要表演《劝世良言五字歌》、《人逢盛世老变少》等新创作或应时现编的节目。

Pingyin Yugu is also called Yugu script. It was once a form of Taoist chanting and later became a form of folk rap, which is an intangible heritage project at the municipal level. The performer plays the clappers and Yugu drum while rapping, generally starting with a prologue of 4 sentences to lead to the main body of the script. Its tunes are lugubrious and vigorous, its lines are easy to understand and the performer is full of passion. In the past, the representative works are as follows: Records of Golden Whip, the Case of Mr. Liu, The Legend of Yue Fei and so on. Nowadays, some newly-created or simultaneously-created works are also popular, such as Song of five-word Lines to Persuade People to Good Deeds and The Old Became Younger in a Prosperous Era.

宋极大鼓

木板大鼓

Muban Dagu (wooden clappers and bass drum)

木板大鼓原是一种穷人讨饭的手段，后来变成一种说唱艺术，民国初年传入济南，现为市级非遗项目。演唱者左手打板，右手持藤棍击鼓，说唱表演。曲目长短篇、小段皆有，如《杨家将》、《隋唐演义》、《林海雪原》、《苦菜花》、《巧劝亲家》、《弯钩锄巧换大盖帽》等。其行腔变化无穷，喜处高亢豪放，悲处委婉苍凉。表演风格幽默风趣，由一人或多人演出都行。

Muban Dagu was once a means of begging, and later became a form of folk rap. It was introduced to Jinan in the early years of The Republic of China (1912-1949), and now it is one of the intangible heritage projects at the municipal level. The performers rap as well as the wooden clappers in the left hand and the drum with a cane stick in the right hand. Their works are of different lengths, such as Generals of the Yang Family, Romance of the Sui and Tang Dynasties, The Forest Sea and Snowfield, Sow Thistle, Successful Persuasion of the Relatives in-laws and so on. The tunes are of great variety, sometimes loud and sonorous, sometimes euphemistic and desolate. The performance, which is humorous and amusing, can be given by one or more people.

其他

「其 他」 Regional Culture of Jinan

千佛山廟會

千佛山庙会

The Temple Fair of Qianfo Mountain

登高远眺

买卖山货

制作糖画

玻璃工艺

游人如潮

曲艺表演

烧香祈福

庙会原是佛、道二教为争夺信众而举行的宗教活动，逐渐演化为民众广泛参与的民俗活动。自唐代始，千佛山庙会每年"九九"重阳节前后都要举行，影响涉及省内外，现为省级非遗项目。庙会期间，民众或阖家出游、登山远眺、赏景抒怀、烧香祈福，或买卖山货、交易杂货、品尝小吃、观赏民俗，饱赏秋日之山景城色，尽享人伦之和谐惬意。庙会持续数日，游者常数万人。

The Temple Fair of Qianfo Mountain is an intangible cultural heritage project at the provincial level. The Temple Fair was once a religious activity hold by Buddhists or Taoists to contest with each other for more believers, and gradually derived into a widely-participated folk activity. Since the Tang Dynasty, the Temple Fair of Qianfo Mountain has yearly taken place around the Double Ninth Festival, known in and out of Shandong Province. During the temple fair, people can have a family outing, climb the mountain to look far into the distance, admire the scenery to express their thoughts and feelings, burn perfumes to ask for blessing, trade mountain products or groceries, taste snacks and enjoy folk culture performances. They can fully enjoy mountain scenery in autumn and have a good time with their family. The temple fair continues several days, entertaining tens of thousands of tourists.

章丘扁鼓

章丘扁鼓

Zhangqiu Biangu

章丘扁鼓是一种民间打击乐形式，据传于明洪武年间从山西传入，遍及全县各地，现为省级非遗项目。鼓呈扁圆弧形，用槐木或枣木等制成，蒙以熟好的牛皮，分为小、中、大、特号。乐队由各号鼓、锣、钹、镲若干组成，演奏分为移动式和固定式，击鼓有单击、双击、滚击、点击和击鼓心、鼓帮、鼓边、飞槌等技巧，曲牌有《九龙翻身》、《狮子滚绣球》、《擂通》等十几种。

As one of the intangible heritage projects at the provincial level, Zhangqiu Biangu is a form of folk percussion music. It is said to have been introduced to Zhangqiu from Shanxi Province in the Ming Dynasty, which is popular all over the county. The drum is oblate and arch-shaped, made of Chinese scholar tree or date wood, covered with processed cowhide (which is very soft and strong). The sizes of the drums are small, medium, large and outsize. The instruments of the band consist of drums of all sizes, gongs, cymbals. The performers are movable or standing at an established place. The ways of beating the drum range from single, double, rolling the drumstick on the drum, beating a certain point, the drum center, the arch-shaped part and the edge and quick and constant handle the drumstick. The Qu tunes amount to more than ten, such as Nine Dragons Turning Over, Lions Rolling a Silk Ball and Leitong Drum.

章丘鐵匠生活習俗

章丘铁匠生活习俗

The Living Custom of Zhangqiu Blacksmiths

章丘自秦汉以来就以出产铁器闻名，明初以打铁为生的手工业户数超过农业户，素有铁匠之乡的美誉，现为省级非遗项目。章丘铁匠技艺高超，以打造农用工具和生活用具为主，也制作建筑配件和特定器具，甚至能打造快枪等新式武器。分为在家收活的铁匠铺和四乡游走的铁匠摊，其生活方式影响甚广。随机器大工业的发展，章丘铁匠正在逐渐消亡。

The living custom of Zhangqiu blacksmiths is a project of intangible cultural heritage at provincial level. Ever since the Qin Dynasty and Han Dynasty, Zhangqiu has been famous for its ironware, and in the Ming Dynasty, the households of handicraftsmen living on forging were more than those of farmers, so Zhangqiu is well-known as the Homeland of Blacksmiths. Zhangqiu blacksmiths are highly skilful, mainly forge farm implements and iron articles of everyday use, and some forge building hardware and specific utensils, some can even make modern weapons, for example, sharp gun. There are two kinds of blacksmiths, some worked at their own smithies at home and the others went out to other places with their migrating stands. The lifestyles of Zhangqiu blacksmiths have a widespread influence. With the development of mechanized industry, the living customs of Zhangqiu Blacksmiths are dying out.

宏济堂传统中药文化

宏济堂传统中药文化

Traditional Chinese Medicine Culture of Hongji Tang

人工选料

古法炮制

手工制丸

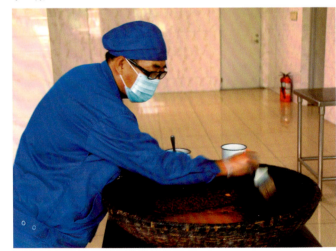

认真化验

检查样品

1907年由乐镜宇创建"乐家老铺济南宏济堂"，1911年建立宏济堂栈房加工中成药，现为省级非遗项目。宏济堂以"宏德广布、济世养生"为理念，继承中国传统医药"货真价实、质量第一"的传统文化，从药材选购的"五不要"（不是一等品、陈货、有杂质、非药用部分、产地不是最佳的不要），到对生产过程和质量的严格控制，一直坚持诚信经营，100多年来从未出现任何质量问题。

Traditional Chinese Medicine Culture of Hongji Tang is a project of intangible cultural heritage at the provincial level. In 1907, Yue Jingyu started Jinan Hongji Tang of the Yues' Old Established Shop. In 1911, Hongji Tang had a warehouse to process Chinese patent drug. Hongji Tang is based on the principles of "spread the good virtue; benefit the age and help keep fit", and inherits traditional Chinese medicine culture of "goods genuine, prices reasonable and quality first". And also Hongji Tang is strict in the selection, purchase and process of the medicinal materials as well as the quality of drugs. Hongji Tang is devoted to honest management for more than one hundred years without any quality problem.

宏济堂园区夜景

大观园晨光茶社

大观园晨光茶社

Chenguang Teahouse in the Grand View Garden

外 观

传承人孙小林在辅导小演员

齐乐

帮带

戏谑

单口

神秘

晨光茶社位于济南市大观园商场内，1943年开业，1966年歇业，2006年重新恢复，现为市级非遗项目。晨光茶社由相声大师孙少林创办，是专门表演相声的演出场所，众多相声名家如张寿臣、马三立、高德明、周德山等先后在晨光茶社表演，培养了如李伯祥、赵振铎、赵文启等新一代相声名家。现在主要以义演的形式培养相声新人，传承济南相声。

Chenguang Teahouse, one municipal project of intangible cultural heritage in Jinan, is located in the Grand View Garden. It was opened in 1943, closed up in 1966 and reopened in 2006. The Teahouse, intended as a place for crosstalk performance, was started by Sun Shaolin, a crosstalk master. Many cross talk masters including zhang Shouchen, Ma Sanli, Gao Deming, Zhou Deshan once performed here and a new generation of cross talk celebrities such as Li Boxiang, Zhao Zhenduo and Zhao Wenqi have been cultivated here. At present, Chenguang Teahouse cultivates crosstalkers and inherits Jinan cross talk by means of charity performance.

后记

　　济南是著名的历史文化名城，非物质文化遗产众多。保存这些世世代代身口相传的地域文化遗产，对于保持我们的文化传统具有重要意义。出版一本图片集，整理记录济南地区的非物质文化遗产，用镜头展现这些弥足珍贵又极易消失的文化瑰宝，是为传承济南地域文化所作的一点贡献。

　　济南地区的非物质文化遗产项目很多，但大量的文学和音乐类项目不便用图片展示，有些可用图片展示的项目在形式上大同小异，加之图集的容量有限，很难用一本图册进行全面展示。因此，作者仅从济南地区内经国家、省、市认定的第1至3批共141个非遗项目中，选取了适合用图片展示的有代表性的58个项目进行拍摄整理。在四年多的时间里，作者直接到现场对53个非遗项目传承单位和传承人进行了访问、拍摄，相关单位和个人提供了5个项目的图片，从而汇集整理成这本图片集。

　　在拍摄整理过程中，得到了有关非遗项目传承单位和传承人，章丘市、平阴县、济阳县、商河县、天桥区、历城区、长清区等县区委政研室和县区文广新局的大力支持帮助；文字说明部分参考了由济南市文化局编纂的《济南非物质文化遗产》（三卷）、张冰著《济南工艺美术史》、非遗传承单位和传承人所提供的资料以及部分网络资料，在此一并表示感谢。因能力和资料所限，出现疏漏错谬亦或难免，敬请读者谅解。

何卫东

2013年4月

《天下泉城·济南非物质文化遗产撷英》编委会

主　任　张福俭

副主任　刘程华　崔　刚

摄　影　何卫东等
撰　稿　何卫东　何睿媞
翻　译　胡丽英　邢俊霞　李学栋　李钰欣
校　译　崔振河

责任编辑　戴梅海
封面设计　何睿媞　张大卫
版式设计　戴梅海

图书在版编目（ＣＩＰ）数据

天下泉城：济南非物质文化遗产撷英 ／ 中共济南市
市委政策研究室，济南市文化广电新闻出版局，济南出版
有限责任公司编. —— 济南：济南出版社，2013.1
　　ISBN 978-7-5488-0755-1

　　Ⅰ．①天… Ⅱ．①中… ②济… ③济… Ⅲ．①文化遗
产－济南市－图集 Ⅳ．①K295.21-64

中国版本图书馆CIP数据核字(2013)第057344号

书　名　天下泉城·济南非物质文化遗产撷英
编　者　中共济南市委政策研究室
　　　　济南市文化广电新闻出版局
　　　　济南出版有限责任公司
出　版　济南出版社
印　刷　山东星海彩印有限公司
规　格　12开（280×250毫米）
印　张　11.5
版　次　2013年4月第1版
印　次　2013年4月第1次印刷
书　号　ISBN 978-7-5488-0755-1
定　价　198.00元